***

HOW RUSSIA ELECTED TRUMP

***

HOW TRUMP
SOLD
AMERICA'S
SECURITY
TO RUSSIA

***

JOHN GILBERT BEAN

johngilbertbean.wordpress.com

SECOND EDITION

Publisher's Cataloging-in-Publication

Bean, John Gilbert, 1933 –

HOW RUSSIA ELECTED TRUMP
HOW TRUMP SOLD AMERICA'S SECURITY TO RUSSIA

/ Maureen Bean – ed.

p. cm.
Includes index
1. DONALD TRUMP   2. NATIONAL SECURITY
3. POLITICS   4. RUSSIAN ESPIONAGE
5. PUTIN   6. BIAS
I. Title

ISBN-13: 978-1727001129
ISBN-10: 172700125

Published by: JOHN GILBERT BEAN PUBLISHING
SAN: 253-0287

951-265-1124

Send comments to: JBeanMBean@msn.com

SECOND EDITION

- A VERY, VERY EXCELLENT BOOK ABOUT PUTIN AND TRUMP -
"ALL MY BOOKS ARE VERY, VERY EXCELLENT."

- A VERY, VERY EXCELLENT BOOK ABOUT PUTIN AND TRUMP -
"ALL MY BOOKS ARE VERY, VERY EXCELLENT."

CONTENTS

CONTENTS (CONTINUED)

CHAPTER 1. INTRODUCTION - WHY THIS BOOK WAS WRITTEN.

By the 2015 presidential election, social media had become a bastion of millions of advocates of special interests of all proclivities which were ripe for exploitation. Some of these are anti-taxes, anti-regulations, anti-black, anti--nonwhite, anti-immigrant, pro-democrat, pro-republican, anti-lesbian, anti-gay, anti-gun control, anti-abortion, anti-government ownership of land, pro-rich, anti-welfare.

For example, on my Wife's Facebook account, one of the most outspoken of the Pro-Republican zealots was a former high-school classmate of mine – Babs (not her real name). With my wife's permission, I wrote to Babs on Facebook. I asked Babs how she could possibly support Trump as he is, in my opinion, pro-rich, a racist bigot, anti-gay, anti-lesbian, anti-immigrant, and anti-transvestite, anti-transsexual. anti-poor, pro-assault weapons, pro-Putin, frequenter-of-prostitutes, and a pathological liar. I meant no unkindness or insult to Babs. I was just trying to find out what goes on in the head of a staunch Trump supporter.

Zounds! Instead of information, I got a bunch of guff from dozens and dozens of angry Trump supporters telling me that "I had insulted Babs, hurt her feelings, and made her so sick she had to take to her bed." Further, they said, per its policies, Facebook cannot not to be used to insult others."

But nobody explained to me how I was insulting Babs and why they were pro Trump – I just asked a question! I believe now some of my critics were Russian pro-trump hackers who flooded my question to Babs with a personal attack on me.

I did not mean to insult Babs. I just asked her simple questions about how she can support someone like Trump. I had hoped for an answer, but I didn't get one!

THE PLEDGE OF ALLEGIANCE TO OUR FLAG:

As Trump should know, the Pledge of Allegiance to our Flag states, America is, "One Nation, under God, with Liberty and Justice for All."

This means equal treatment under the law for all regardless of race, color, creed, national origin, sexual orientation, politics, or other biases. Trump doesn't want that! Babs doesn't want that! Many republicans and many, many others don't want that!

PRESIDENT OBAMA WANTED THAT AND BROUGHT AMERICA CLOSER TO ACHIEVING IT.

I WANT THAT! THAT'S WHY THIS BOOK WAS WRITTEN!

CHAPTER 2. BEAN'S LAW OF DEMOCRATIC ELECTIONS – HOW TRUMP WAS ELECTED BY PUTIN AND BIASED VOTERS.

Most democratic elections are fairly close. Usually, there are two fairly closely matched sides as no one wants to spend money on an election where their side or position or candidate has little or no chance of winning. Each side in most close elections is thus assured of about 1/3 of the votes. All that is necessary to win is receive 1/6 of the remaining 1/3 (2/6) of the total votes plus 1 more vote to win with a majority of at least 1 vote - one more than half of the votes.

   1/3 + 1/6 = 3/6 = ½ = 50 Percent WITH ONE MORE VOTE NEEDED TO WIN.

Putin's plan to elect Trump was simple. He spent almost a billion dollars to hack American social media in order to find and fuel the biases of as many of the potential voters as possible. Putin knew that if he could influence highly biased voters that Trump was the candidate favorable to their biases, no matter how obscene their biases, he could elect Donald Trump – THE CANDIDATE OF THEIR BIAS. Then, Putin's hackers went to work to make sure voters saw information that favored their biases and prejudices: Trump over Hillary Clinton. It made no difference if the information sent out to Americans was truthful or not, just that it played to their biased pro-Trump prejudices. Regardless, it worked for Russia. Trump was elected.

Every Reader knows how biases affect voters. Many of you know, for example, your parents have always voted Republican or Democratic. If your parents were republican, and if Satan were running as a republican and Jesus or Mohammad as a democrat, your parents would vote republican because they always do.

In this election, Russian hackers painted Trump as the candidate of your strongly held biases knowing you would vote for Trump no matter how terrible a person he was otherwise. And Trump is a very, very terrible person – go back and read chapter 1 again.

Based on my experience in working with the mentally ill, Trump seems to be mentally ill. He seems unable to focus and has trouble reading than about half a page at a time. He is a pathological liar. Trump often describes events only as Excellent, Very Excellent, and Very, Very Excellent.

Nevertheless, Voters elected Trump with all his biases and prejudices.

Here is the problem with electing Trump with all his bias and prejudices. Read the Pledge of Allegiance again in Chapter 1:

"One Nation, under God, with Liberty and Justice for All." This means equal treatment under the law for all regardless of race, color, creed, national origin, sexual orientation, politics, or other biases. Trump doesn't want that! Many Republicans don't want that and appoint judges that don't want that. Trump should be our example and leader. Instead he is a disgrace!

I HAD TO DO SOMETHING – HENCE THIS BOOK.

CHAPTER 3. LIAR TRUMP.

During the presidential election campaign, Trump and other republicans addressed Hillary Clinton as "Crooked Hillary" as they were perhaps programmed to do by Russian intelligence agents. First of all, Hillary Clinton is not crooked. Second, Trump _is_ a pathological liar as has been widely reported on the TV and in the press.

 Since Trump addressed Hillary using a slur, it is only fair and some payback to address Trump in this book as "Liar Trump."

Below, Trumps lying and some other facets of his conduct and behavior are satirized and characterized.

What does Trump call America's most deadly enemy Putin? Answer: "sir."

What does Trump say when America's most deadly enemy Putin speaks? Answer: "Yes sir."

What does Trump do when he talks? Answer: "Lie, Lie, Lie."

What does Trump say to a prostitute?

Answer: "Don't tell anyone. My lawyer has a check for you."

What does Trump say when America's most deadly enemy Putin whispered in his ear for him to double the price of crude oil?
**Answer: "Yes Sir." …   Then Trump gave Putin a $900 billion gift!!!!
– See chapter 6.**

CHAPTER 4. RUSSIA, CHINA, AND NORTH KOREA ARE DEADLY ENEMIES OF AMERICA.

Make no mistake: Russia, China, and North Korea are deadly enemies of America. In 1945, Russia attempted to retain Eastern Europe territory it seized from Germany during WWII, but was thwarted when America's Berlin Blockade forced Russia out of Eastern Europe.

 In June, 1950, Russia, China, and North Korea attacked South Korea and America during the Korean War. Thanks to General Douglas MacArthur leading the American Army, the Marine Corps (of which I was a member), and US AirPower, the axis powers were forced out of South Korea and back across the Yalu River.

General MacArthur wanted to invade China, but fortunately, President Truman wouldn't let him.

- A VERY, VERY EXCELLENT BOOK ABOUT PUTIN AND TRUMP -
"ALL MY BOOKS ARE VERY, VERY EXCELLENT."

In 2014 Russia invaded Eastern Europe to steal territory there but was forced back of out of Ukraine and other stolen territory by America except for the Crimea which Russia has taken completely over.

 RUSSIA IS A VERY POOR COUNTRY EVEN THOUGH IT IS RICH IN NATURAL RESOURCES - ALL EXCEPT CRUDE OIL ARE TOO EXPENSIVE TO EXPLOIT.

BEFORE TRUMP, INTERNATIONAL AGREEMENTS KEPT THE PRICE OF CRUDE OIL ROCK-BOTTOM LOW.   BECAUSE RUSSIA IS A VERY POOR COUNTRY AND CRUDE OIL IS RUSSIA'S MAIN SOURCE OF INCOME TO BUILD WEAPONS,   ANY INCREASE IN CRUDE OIL PRICE IS USED BY RUSSIA TO BUILD HYDROGEN BOMBS AND MISSILES THAT ONE DAY MAY BE USED IN AN ATTEMPT TO DESTROY AMERICA.

CHAPTER 5.   PUTIN SPENT UPWARDS OF A BILLION DOLLARS TO ELECT TRUMP.

Hopefully, most Americans watched the CNN Special on Putin. CNN has the goods on Putin and Russia.   Putin spent upwards of a billion dollars to get Trump elected and become his Best Friend.

 Your personal and private computer information was stolen and used to benefit Trump. Your email address and postings on Twitter, Facebook, and other social media were hacked and stolen.

Everything on Hillary Clinton's private computers was hacked and stolen.

All this information was read and evaluated by Russian spies expert in American culture.

Then using your stolen personal information, you were fed phony information claiming that Liar Trump supported your feelings, values, beliefs, and desires. And then because you were tricked by this treachery, many of you voted for Trump and got him elected.

- A VERY, VERY EXCELLENT BOOK ABOUT PUTIN AND TRUMP -
"ALL MY BOOKS ARE VERY, VERY EXCELLENT."

Since CNN has published in detail the facts of Putin's interference in
our presidential election which got Trump elected, this matter will not
be discussed further in this book.
BE SURE TO VIEW SEE THIS CNN EXPOSE' IF YOU HAVEN'T WATCHED
IT ALREADY!

NOTE: TRUMP AND PUTIN HAVE NOT RELEASED ANY SIGNIFICANT
INFORMATION ABOUT AGREEMENTS FROM THEIR MEETINGS, TELEPHONE
DISCUSSIONS, AND ELECTRONIC COMMUNICATIONS. IN THE FOLLOWING
CHAPTERS, I SURMISED TO THE BEST OF MY ABILITY AS TO WHAT THEY AGREED
TO DO BASED ON EVENTS THAT FOLLOWED THEIR MEETINGS – SPECIFICALLY, A
DRASTIC INCREASE IN CRUDE OIL PRICE.

IF TRUMP DOESN'T LIKE MY ASSUMPTIONS, THEN HE SHOULD
RELEASE WRITTEN MINUTES OF ALL THEIR DISCOURSE AND
AGREEMENTS: IF I AM WRONG I WILL APOLOGIZE AND MAKE
IMMEDIATE CORRECTIONS TO THIS BOOK. (BUT, I DON'T THINK HE
WILL.)

CHAPTER 6.   TRUMP'S $900 BILLION PAYMENT TO PUTIN FOR GETTING HIM ELECTED.

PUTIN WAS FORCED TO PUT HIS EXPANSION PLANS ON HOLD AGAIN WHEN AMERICA *ANNOUNCED THAT THE B-2 STEALTH BOMBER WAS OPERATIONAL.*

I WAS AT FIRST FLIGHT OF THE B-2 ON JULY 17, 1989.

 RUSSIA'S EXPENSIVE THEN NEW AIR DEFENSE SYSTEM WAS VALUELESS TO DEFEND AGAINST THE B-2.   RUSSIA, BEING A POOR COUNTRY, COULD NOT AFFORD TO RAPIDLY UPGRADE TO ANOTHER NEW AIR DEFENSE SYSTEM.

FORTUNATELY, CRUDE OIL PRICES WERE KEPT LOW CAUSING RUSSIA GREAT DIFFICULTY IN OBTAINING REQUIRED FUNDS TO BUILD SUPER WEAPONS AND UP-GRADE TO AN EFFECTIVE AIR DEFENSE SYSTEM.

BUT NOW, AFTER HIS ELECTION, TRUMP ALLOWED A DRASTIC INCREASE IN INTERNATIONAL CRUDE OIL PRICES AT RUSSIAN BEHEST. AS A RESULT, RUSSIA WILL MAKE TRILLIONS OF DOLLARS SELLING CRUDE OIL AT INFLATED PRICES.

Trump's close relationship with Putin who got him elected has cost every family in America about $1200 per year because of the huge increase in crude oil prices which have drastically raised gasoline prices at the pump. This enormous gift to Russia costs 125 million American families annually $150, 000, 000, 000 ($150 billion per year), $900 billion over 6 years that goes directly into Putin's pockets (and Putin is already the richest person in the world).

Just in this last year, the price of crude oil has continued to increase and has raised the price of gasoline by one dollar per gallon.

Worst of all**!!!!!** Now Putin has the funds needed to accelerate Russian weapons development and territorial expansion. Trump has also wrongfully lined his pockets by raising oil prices which inflated the value of his stock holdings in Shell, Exxon, and Mobil

. Has Trump done anything illegal? I don't know. I am just a reporter of the facts to the best of my knowledge and ability.

I do think what Trump has done is wrong. It's for the FBI to determine if anything he has done is illegal.

CHAPTER 7.

WHAT SHOULD AMERICA DO NOW?

- Trump was elected by the voters because of Russian treachery.

THERE WAS ELECTION FRAUD. THE FRAUD WAS PERPETRATED ON THE VOTERS BY THE RUSSIANS BEFORE AMERICAN VOTERS WENT TO THE POLLS.

 NOW IS THE TIME TO MAKE SURE SUCH A TRAVESTY NEVER HAPPENS AGAIN:

- Russian agents still in America should be arrested and charged with unlawful hacking.

- DIPLOMATIC RELATIONS with Russia should be immediately terminated.

- Putin should be declared persona non grata and never be allowed in America again.

- A VERY, VERY EXCELLENT BOOK ABOUT PUTIN AND TRUMP -
"ALL MY BOOKS ARE VERY, VERY EXCELLENT."

- TRUMP SHOULD APOLOGIZE TO AMERICA FOR PUTIN'S FOUL DEEDS AND ADMIT ANY PERSONAL COMPLICITY AND KNOWLEDGE.

- DIRECTOR OF THE FBI AND OTHER RESPONSIBLE FEDERAL OFFICIALS SHOULD DETERMINE HOW RUSSIAN HACKING WAS ALLOWED TO OCCUR, AND WHY FOREIGN AGENTS WERE NOT PREVENTED FROM INTERFERING WITH AMERICA'S PRESIDENTIAL ELECTION.

- CRUDE OIL PRICES SHOULD BE SET BELOW $30 A BARREL FOR THE NEXT 10 YEARS SO RUSSIA CANNOT CONTINUE TO RECEIVE ILL-GOTTEN GAINS DUE TO LIAR TRUMP ENABLING CRUDE OIL PRICE TO INCREASE.

CHAPTER 8. EPILOGUE.

TRUMP FANS : THE JOKE'S ON YOU!

TRUMP FANS: I FEEL A DUTY AS AN AMERICAN TO EXPOSE LIAR TRUMP AND ENEMY PUTIN IN THE PREVIOUS CHAPTERS.

But non-millionaire Trump fans, the Joke's on you! You got who and what you voted for:

YOU GOT DONALD TRUMP!

Trump has forgotten you, but Trump gave the very rich including himself a very big stock price increase on their stock holdings by making a whopping tax cut tax on corporate profits. This sent stocks soaring as all this tax cut then went into corporate profits.

WHERE DID TRUMP GET THE MONEY TO DO THIS? SIMPLE, HE GOT IT BY INCREASING THE NATIONAL DEBT WHICH YOU HAVE TO PAY WITH YOUR INCOME TAX INCLUDING THE ANNUAL INTEREST ON IT.   SO ENJOY THE INCREASE IN YOUR INCOME TAX.   THE JOKE'S ON YOU! IF YOU DON'T BELIEVE ME, ASK YOUR ACCOUNTANT. YOU ALSO WILL PAY AS THE COST OF LIVING WILL GREATLY INCREASE.

SPEAKING OF COST OF LIVING, HOW ARE YOU ENJOYING TRUMP'S GIFT TO ENEMY PUTIN OF A WHOPPING INCREASE IN THE PRICE OF CRUDE OIL WHICH IS PUTIN'S MAIN EXPORT. UNFORTUNATELY, CRUDE OIL IS ESSENTIAL TO MAKE YOUR GASOLINE AND THE CRUDE OIL PRICE INCREASE HAS SENT THE PRICE YOU PAY FOR YOUR GASOLINE SOARING WHILE ENEMY PUTIN ROLLS ON THE FLOOR LAUGHING AT TRUMP'S STUPIDITY.

CHAPTER 8. EPILOGUE (CONTINUED).

TRUMP FANS : BIGOTRY AND DISCRIMINATION ARE UN-AMERICAN

Every American knows the Pledge of Allegiance to our Flag states

America is, "One Nation, under God, with Liberty and Justice for All."

It's terrible some of you Trump fans support Trump's disgusting bigotry and discrimination of many, many, many loyal Americans who work hard, obey the law, and pay taxes but through no fault of their own are a minority of some kind: born non-white, born Gay, born Lesbian, born Trans-Sexual, born Bi-Sexual, born non-Christian, or born with serious handicap. These people were born the way they are just like most others were born male, or born female, or born Christian.

Like other citizens, minority citizens are Human Beings and loyal American citizens! They all always deserve to be treated with respect!

The results of scientific studies are crystal clear: You can't change the sexual identity you were born with. You can't change your inborn sexual orientation. Many, many try or are forced to try - with very, very little or no success, but many, many have ruined their bodies, ruined their lives, and have experienced very great unhappiness.

Every American citizen always deserves to be treated with respect - regardless of their race, color, creed, national origin, sexual orientation, or religious beliefs,

If two gays wish to marry, then a baker should say to himself, "My religion and beliefs prohibit Gay Marriage for me, but their religion and beliefs and happiness permit it, and it is essential for them, so I will respect their religion and beliefs just like I expect them to respect me and mine - I will bake their cake just the way they want it baked."

CHAPTER 9. FINALLY.

Putin-Lover Trump: YOU ARE A BIGOT AND HAVE SOLD OUT OUR AMERICA TO THE RUSSIANS."

REPUBLICANS AND BIGOTS: PUTIN AND THE RUSSIANS HACKED INTO YOUR COMPUTERS AND OTHERWISE LEARNED OF YOUR PREJUDICES: WHETHER YOU WERE ANTI-GAY, ANTI-LESBIAN, ANTI-NON-WHITE, ANTI-BISEXUAL, ANTI-NON-CHRISTIAN, ANTI-POOR, ANTI-GUN CONTROL, OR ANTI-WHATEVER AND THEN MADE SURE YOU THOUGHT TRUMP WAS YOUR HERO SO YOU WOULD MAKE EXTRA EFFORT TO VOTE FOR BIGOT TRUMP.

- A VERY, VERY EXCELLENT BOOK ABOUT PUTIN AND TRUMP -
"ALL MY BOOKS ARE VERY, VERY EXCELLENT."

AND FINALLY:

HILLARY RAN AN ELECTION CAMPAIGN THAT WORRIED ABOUT WHAT TRUMP SAID ABOUT HER ("I HAVEN'T DONE ANYTHING WRONG.") INSTEAD OF BLASTING BIGOT TRUMP.

TOO BAD! HILLARY WOULD HAVE BEEN A GREAT PRESIDENT FOR ALL AMERICANS - JUST LIKE OBAMA.

NOW, TRUMP IS SO LOONY THAT HE IS TRYING TO UNDO ALL THE GREAT LEGISLATION PASSED BY PRESIDENT OBAMA.

FORTUNATELY, IT IS JUST A MATTER OF TIME THAT OBAMA'S LEGISLATION AND LEGACY WILL BE TOTALLY RESTORED.

OBAMA WILL ALWAYS BE REMEMBERED AS ONE OF AMERICA'S GREATEST PRESIDENTS.

LIAR TRUMP WILL ALWAYS BE REMEMBERED AS AMERICA'S WORST PRESIDENT.

JGB

9 781727 001129